SENIOR ORPHANS

SURVIVAL SKILLS

SENIOR ORPHANS: SURVIVAL SKILLS

Cover and interior design by Sue Balcer

ISBN: 9781698127521

SENIOR ORPHANS

Sunie Levin, M.Ed.

FOR MY HUSBAND
WHO HATES TO HEAR ME KVETCH.......

"Age is an issue of mind over matter.
If you don't mind, it doesn't matter"

Mark Twain

Books also by Sunie Levin

You and Your Grandchild: Special Ways To Keep In Touch

Mingled Roots: A Guide For Grandparents of Interfaith Grandchildren

Make New Friends Live Longer: A Guide For Seniors

Ready or Not Here I Come: How To Choose Your Best Retirement Community

TABLE OF CONTENTS

PART II—DEALING WITH COMMON PROBLEMS

Part III

Part IV

PART I

INTRODUCTION

ARE YOU A SENIOR ORPHAN?

My husband wanted me to title this book "*Growing Old Sucks.*" He was serious. Perhaps he was right. The Victorian Robert Browning said in one of his verses, "Grow old along with me. The best is yet to be. The last of life, for which the first was made." Easy for him to say! He was only fifty two when he penned those lines. I decided that I was going to prove to my husband that growing old has wonderful possibilities.

So who is a senior? Some consider themselves seniors at age fifty, that way they can start getting perks from AARP, restaurants, airlines and movie theaters. My husband wouldn't admit to being a senior until his first grandchild was born. He wouldn't say he was a senior, but he liked the title of "grandpa."

Then who are Senior Orphans? It is a situation, not an arbitrary age. There are thirteen million seniors in America living alone, single, widowed, divorced with no advocate, who have to make their own decisions. If they have children, none of them live in the same city where the senior lives. Or they may be estranged. They have their own lives to live. And the seniors old friends, if they haven't died, have their own problems to deal with. As my husband often says, we have more friends in the cemetery than we have above ground. Having children or being married will not make us safe from being a senior orphan. We can all become Senior Orphans, you can outlive your husband or wife and not have a partner. Many seniors live isolated without support of either family or friends.

The movie actress Bette Davis famously said "Growing old is not for sissies." I won't argue with her. I am eighty-eight years old, so I know what she is talking about. I visit doctors so often that when my friends can't get in to see theirs, they call me. They figure that no matter the complaint, I've had it.

I lost my rose-colored glasses decades ago. I am not going to try to beguile you into thinking that this book will give you a magic formula for making aging easy. But I can give senior orphans all sorts of ways to help themselves.

Who am I to be giving advice? Good question. I am a life-long educator and have written several self-help books. I have become a syndicated newspaper columnist with interviews on radio and T.V. shows and have lectured on many major cruise lines.

I like to plan ahead and know what options are available, instead of waiting until a crisis, then making a decision that turns out to be disaster. Life changes, often in the blink of an eye. We become alone. But that doesn't mean we need to become isolated. It's something that is allowed to happen.

So, if you are a senior orphan, lonely in your apartment or retirement community with no one readily available for support if needed, there are things you can do to make your life more pleasant, more safe and more meaningful. You may have to be alone, but you don't have to be lonely. It's totally up to you.

The purpose of this book is to provide information and a guide to available resources that can help Senior Orphans deal with their situation and to take action to improve it. If even one of these suggestions proves to be of value to you. I have accomplished my objective.

Keep in mind that if you stop kvetching (complaining) and use chutzpah (lots of nerve) you can improve the quality of your life enormously.

SO WHAT'S THE PROBLEM?

Things change at warp speed. Seniors used to be looked up to as repositories of wisdom. Nowadays, we are usually perceived as being obsolete, unable to cope with the pace of modern life. This actually in some ways is true. It is startling to see three-year-olds nimbly using their fingers to play with computers while we barely know how to use e-mail on the computer.

I hate statistics. They're boring. But, reluctantly, I'm going to give you a few because I think they're meaningful. When I looked them up, they startled me. Nearly half of adults over sixty-five are divorced, separated or widowed. That's a lot of people living alone. Meanwhile, the elder population is growing because people are living longer.

Almost 20% of baby boomers do not have children. While this is happening, nearly eighty million millennials are delaying marriage and many are choosing to remain childless. This is their choice and works well for a while, until they too become seniors. This is going to increase the number of Senior Orphans. Their choice will catch up with them, and what will they do when they have absolutely no one that cares about them?

More and more seniors are aging without a family support system. It used to be that families stayed together, in the same city or town—even in the same house. Society is mobile now. It's actually rather rare for children to stay in the same city as their parents or even live in the same country.

Things change drastically as we age. It's difficult to cope with things that once were so easy we scarcely thought about them. For example:

- Taking pills on time
- Sticking with a treatment plan and filling needed prescriptions
- Seeing a physician when needed
- Performing everyday tasks like dressing, cooking meals, doing laundry
- Driving to appointments, getting groceries
- Answering telephones and understanding message
- Maintaining balance avoiding falls
- Opening jars or packages
- Paying bills and finances when cognition declines

This may not be a pretty picture, but it's reality. It's what Senior Orphans face every day. What can be done? Well, that's exactly what this book is all about.

"We're born alone, we die alone. Only through our love and friendship can we create the illusion for the moment that we're not alone."

— Orson Welles

HOW TO PREPARE FOR LIVING SOLO

Staying at home is one option. "Aging in place" the government likes to call it. It has its pluses—and minuses. Quite often it requires a home health caregiver, that is, if you find one that is compatible and you can afford to pay. If you want to age in place in your own home, think about making modifications that will keep you safe and comfortable. Later in this book I will describe smart home technology that can help. If you feel isolated and lonely there are alternatives.

If you don't want a stranger in the house with you, or simply can't afford one, staying in your home is challenging. If you fall, there is no one around to call the paramedics. You can buy a fall alert that you can wear on your wrist or around your neck. Don't forget another important factor if you choose to stay in your home alone, there is no one sitting at the dinner table for conversation or companionship.

Some baby boomers are looking at senior cohousing, normally condominiums or individual housing units. All have a common house with kitchen and spaces for meetings and socializing. Being part of a community offers support that can have a positive impact on health and social connection during later years.

Another alternative is to move into a continuing care retirement community. These can be expensive. But there will be new friends to make, people to interact with, daily activities to give you exercise and keep your mind stimulated, meals prepared and dining rooms where you can share with others. As you need more care, it is available. Some are rental facilities, while others require a buy-in. You are going to be there for the rest of your life, so you want to chose wisely. Don't wait too long so you can enjoy it while you still have your health.

Dr. Sosland says we have to be careful that bullying is a real problem in senior adult population. From excluding others from activities to name calling to physical altercations it needs to be taken seriously. Retirement homes, nursing homes and senior centers have introduced programs and policies to curb bullying. It is important to report such behavior to professionals.

"If you don't like something, change it.
If you can't change it, change your attitude.
Don't complain."

— Maya Angelou poet

STOP KVETCHING ALREADY

Kvetch and you'll lose your friends. Charlie is a constant complainer. You know the type. Oh boy, do you know! He's the type of guy that people of a certain age used to refer to as enjoying ill-health. With Charlie, it's always something. "I have this pain in my neck, or I have an allergy to dust." Always something!

He thinks by constantly complaining, people will have sympathy for him. Well, it doesn't work that way. They don't. They resent the constant daily whining. Nobody wants to be around him. Who needs it? People have their own health problems; they really don't want to hear about anybody else's. When they see Charlie at a party, they try to avoid him. Even his wife rolls her eyes when he starts with his list of complaints. What's the point of kvetching anyway? It doesn't make the problem go away.

When you meet Alice, with her constant "organ recital" you try to run in the opposite direction if you can get away fast enough. Alice has never had a meal that she hasn't complained about or sent back. She complains that no one calls her. Big surprise. Who wants to listen to her? It is easier to write her an e-mail.

Psychologists call it "chronic kvetching syndrome." They really do. It is a condition marked by constant complaints to anyone who will listen about anything and everything that comes into the kvetcher's mind.

Some people talk to their hairstylist moaning about all their perceived annoyances. At least the stylist gets paid for listening. Some people strike up a conversation with perfect strangers to complain about the weather and what a terrible day they have had. Even if they have a nice day, it doesn't stop them from complaining anyway.

When you see someone you often say "how are you" or "how have you been?" Most of the time, you really don't want to know. It is a rhetorical question. So when someone asks you, what makes you think other people want to hear your kvetches? When you start to kvetch, stop. Nobody wants to hear it. After all, you're trying to make friends, not drive them away.

"It's Never Too Late To Be What You Might Have Been"

— George Elliot

EVERY SENIOR NEEDS CHUTZPAH

I was born with chutzpah. So were you. So was every kid. When I wanted something, I screamed and wailed and kicked until I got it. If I didn't get it fast enough, I kept it up until I did. What else is a kid going to do? But eventually we become civilized. At least most of us.

Chutzpah is hard to define, but you know it when you see it. It's a wonderful Yiddish word, an amalgam of supreme self-confidence, nerve, gall, unwavering determination and never taking no for an answer.

Seniors often feel that younger people lack respect and are patronizing toward them, and at times are being ignored or bullied by them. But we do grow old, and we get pushed around and marginalized unless we stick up for ourselves. Speak up! If you say "I'm too polite or too old" you're going to miss out. But if you say "Yes, I can. Why not? What's to lose by trying?" Then you have chutzpah.

Don't let yourself be pushed around. Chutzpah can be a tricky thing. It doesn't mean being obnoxious. It does mean being self-assertive and persistent. Most of it has to do with attitude. If you don't stand up for yourself, you're going to be pushed around. Be polite, but be firm. If the doctor's staff is dismissive, don't let them put you off. The same holds for merchants, repairmen and people who crowd in front of you at the grocery store. I'm talking about not being a pushover. Especially never take any physical or verbal abuse from anyone. Don't be afraid to speak up for what you feel is right. And if you are certain you are correct, when you get a 'no' continue up the chain of command until you get a 'yes'. Nobody became famous by being passive. It takes chutzpah to keep moving forward to get what you need in life.

"Aging is not lost youth but a new stage of opportunity and strength"

— **Betty Friedan**

NEVER RETIRE FROM LIFE

By the time we're seniors, we fall into a rut. No, it's worse than that. What we fall into is more like a deep trench. Especially after retiring we become set in our ways. Changing our ways at this stage of the game might not seem worth the effort. With the finish line approaching so rapidly, what's the point?

Well, that's one way of looking at it. The other way is to acknowledge that every single day that passes is a pure waste if we are not doing something to enjoy and feel good about . A wasted day is gone forever.

I know it can be difficult to summon the energy to do some of the things I recommend. It isn't easy for me either. But sitting in your room watching your life go by isn't a very appetizing alternative. It's time to think—really think about what you would like to do to make the rest of your life happier and better. Carpe diem. Seize the day.

You think I'm nagging, don't you? Well, I am. The woods (and more probably, the retirement homes) are filled with mega-elders who have continued to lead exceptionally fascinating lives.

Dr. Ruth Westheimer, who is ninety, was an orphan of the Holocaust, a sniper for the Israeli underground, seriously wounded, married three times, all before becoming "Dr. Ruth," known for sexology. She teaches at her alma mater, Columbia Teachers College. And she still is a television personality. When asked if she was ready to retire, the answer was a loud and fervent "No! Not as long as I can keep experiencing the most I can out of life, the better my life is."

Some convince themselves that they are too old and bow out too soon and just watch the world go by. Let go of who you were and be who you are today. Count your blessings.

This is the time to move forward and let go of old fears and self-limiting ideas about age. View this time of your life as a golden opportunity to reimagine what you may want to do for the rest of your life.

"Life Begins At The End Of Your Comfort Zone"

— **Neale Donald Walsch**

REINVENT YOURSELF

My cousin Sondra is one of the wisest and most resilient people I know. Her life has been amazing and I asked her to help me with this particular topic. Below is her words on the subject and I don't think anyone could possibly say them better.

"I was widowed when I was forty two after my first husband died following a four year bout with a rare illness. One thing we did during those four years was to talk about what I would do after he died. We had teenage children, and we agreed that I should not uproot them during their school years, but once they went off to college, I should reinvent myself and start a new life.

After I thought about my life I identified things I was willing to try, and some areas of comfort that I couldn't live without. Once the childrens' needs were taken care of, I was free to reach out and find new opportunities, and the reinvention began.

Since then, I had a twelve year career as a convenience store inspector, a second and third marriage, a career as an executive income tax professional, served seven years as the chairman of our neighborhood committee, taught classes to help new widows start life again, and embarked on a career as a lecturer on cruise ships. I taught myself photography and genealogy and I still have the energy and ability to play golf four times a week at age eighty two.

All of this because I know that every time one door closes, another will open and I need to analyze, reinvent and walk through it. Not everything worked, but with each success, I got better at believing in reinvention. Most important was the help I had along the way. I no longer wait for someone to reach out and pull me in. I have learned to reach out and find those who will reach back.

There is nothing worse than sitting home and knitting in front of the TV because you have nowhere else to go. There is nothing better than sitting home and knitting in front of the TV because that's what you need right now and that's what you choose to do this evening. Analyze and reinvent.

A wise Rabbi from my youth once said about practicing religion that you should do as much as you find comfortable, and then one thing more. It's important that you reach out to do that one thing more that goes just beyond your comfort level—that becomes the basis for a reinvention.

I know now that who I am today is not who I will be six months from now and I look forward to new challenges with the confidence that I can meet them. That being said, if there are times I cannot meet them, I have built a support system of family and friends who will be there for me until I can. Either way, I will continue to analyze and reinvent."

"We need old friends to help us grow old and new friends to help us stay young."

— Letty Cottin Pogrebin

WE ARE NEVER TOO OLD TO MAKE NEW FRIENDS

Eight years ago my oldest daughter informed me, "you know mom, eighty is actually is today's sixty." Now the studies are saying ninety is today's eighty.

You are never too old to make new friends. Living as I do in a retirement community, I frequently hear "it's too hard to make new friends." (Kvetching again.) Seniors say cliques have already formed and nobody wants to allow a new person in. They say all of their old friends have either died or moved away. They say everybody is snobbish.

They are lonesome. And you know what, it's their own fault. Old friends die or move away or grow ill. They are understandably lonesome, but lack the initiative to try and do something about it. There are new friends to be made, but you need to be pro-active in finding them.

There are plenty of studies that demonstrate a lack of friends in one's senior years can sap the life out of anyone.

As we grow older, lifestyle changes are forced on us whether we like them or not. Perhaps a spouse dies. Our health and our mobility are no longer what they used to be. We can become housebound. Some are out of the habit of reaching out to people. Most seniors are in the same boat. They want companionship, too. Friends can help us live longer and better.

We need to scour community newsletters, join book groups, invite new neighbors over for meals. Few will resist the invitation. Ask advice about their doctors and beauticians, sign up with volunteer organizations and take classes. We need to project a sunny disposition and avoid turning people off by complaining. Most importantly, we need to become good listeners; there will be plenty of times when we need someone to really listen to us. Friendships requires the willingness to make the first move in regard to establishing new connections.

Establishing relationships with new people means being able to remember their names, how to contact them and something about their interests. People are delighted when you remember things about them. Writing things down is a good way to remember.

Try social networking. Today's communication technologies can help fill our lives with new relationships. Using e-mail helps maintain established relationships with old friends while building new ones. Making new friends requires being proactive in looking for them. Many seniors are in the same boat, but aren't willing to make the effort to meet new people. Consider attending religious service, taking a class at the library, playing cards and games, joining a singing group, visiting a senior center—-anything that will offer you repeated exposure to a new group of people.

Building strong relationships helps your brain stay active and can help keep dementia at bay. If you are around someone who feels passionate about the same topics, but doesn't agree with your opinion (and can debate in a respectful manner) you're even luckier. Healthy debate and critical thinking are important for all ages.

When Louis Armstrong sang, "When you're smiling, the whole world smiles with you" he didn't know that scientists would one day back up his claim. When you smile it is difficult for others not to smile back. Give it a try.

"We don't stop playing because we grow old. We grow old because we stop playing."

— George Bernard Shaw

MAKE YOUNGER FRIENDS

I've just told you how to start making new friends your age, and acknowledged it might be difficult. Now I'm suggesting making younger friends. Am I serious? Well, as a matter of fact, I am.

It is doable. At age eighty-eight, I have made friends who are ten to twenty years younger. Of course, I could be fooling myself, but they seem to enjoy my company and I certainly enjoy being with them. How has this happened? Some probably look at me as a mom figure and seek advice. Most are simply younger friends we've met along the way and my husband and I enjoy social holidays with them.

So how have I been able to make friends with these younger people? Truth be told, I really haven't done this as a result of any deliberate plan. It just happened. I put myself into environments where younger people were present, like exercise and art classes. For whatever reason there was sufficient rapport for a real bond to happen.

I'm always willing to try new things. Well, that's not totally true. That doesn't include bungee jumping, sky diving or white river rafting. I am interested in people and curious about everything in the world. A son-in-law teases me that I would be interested in land fills. You betcha.

Most of all I'm interested in people of all ages. My husband can't believe I find out so much about a person I have just met, someone in the grocery store, beauty shop, doctor's office. I ask questions. I'm not nosy, I really am interested. Most people are delighted to talk to you; they enjoy talking about their hobbies, travel, kids and their grandchildren. Of course, you may meet the occasional grouch, but that goes with the territory.

After a certain age, how old you are doesn't matter. It helps that both my husband and I feel twenty years younger than we actually are. At least we think so. It's not age, but attitude that makes the difference in acquiring younger friends.

You can always sense it--that instant feeling of rapport, that here is someone I'd like to know better, who seems to be on the same wave-length. When it happens, don't hesitate to tell the person that you feel good about and would like to spend time getting to know him/her.

Making younger friends opens new vistas to explore. It gives you a new perspective on life. Hopefully that makes me more interesting. The added benefit is that it will keep you healthier and less concerned about your daily kvetches.

Every week there are people I knew in my community who died. That's just the way it is. It's why I go out of my way to acquire new younger friends. It gives them the benefit of seeing a road map for when they get older. It gives you the benefit of being friends with someone who drives at night! Making younger friends is a win-win.

Attitude is a little thing that makes a big difference

— Winston Churchill

AGE IS A STATE OF MIND

Age is real. All of us, with our aches and pains know that age is real. Wishing it weren't so changes nothing. By the same token, age is no excuse for pulling back into your shell and becoming a hermit.

Optimism is good for you. Harvard University studies report that the optimist recovers faster from illness and often lives longer. So changing your outlook is extremely important. Looking at each new day as an opportunity instead of a burden to be endured can do wonders. Instead of concentrating on your aches and pains, before going to bed at night think about all the things you are going to do tomorrow. Live your life to the fullest. Find creative activities that make you happy.

My friend Shirley is ninety-four. She is always ready for something new—a new book, a new idea a new friend. She welcomes anything innovative, including the computer. Her curiosity is insatiable. Well beyond an age when many begin to turn away from all things different or unfamiliar, she welcomes nearly everything innovative.

When she lies in bed, she exercises her mind mentally with songs and poems. She enjoys a game of bridge and volunteers at one of the retirement centers to help others learn the game. She felt that it was important to learn something new every day, so she has taken up playing pool. What a superb role model!

My aunt Rose at ninety-one was writing poetry for people she met who helped her at the bank or the doctors she went to see. Her arthritis made it difficult for her to write so she used a digital recorder and her daughter typed and mailed poems for her. She wrote until the day she died.

Anna, one of my friend's mother, had the motto. "live your life like you are going to live forever." At ninety-five she bought a new car and took out a 5 year warranty. She did because she was optimistic she would need it.

"The greatest gift of life is friendship, and I have received it."

— Hubert H. Humphrey

NETWORKING HELPS FIND FRIENDS

Most men are loners. When they make a phone call they state their business in sixty seconds or less, then hang up. On the other hand, women can talk on the phone quite literally for hours. They help each other in time of need, whether a home-cooked meal or just spending time together. For women having a girlfriend network is important for future happiness.

Women are more receptive to sharing their feelings. They feel comfortable opening up to other women for advice. Girlfriends can often work together to improve their lives and lives of those around them. Women enjoy having fun together. They can go out shopping or watch a movie together. They are a sounding board to share feelings and emotions. They are a help to deal with stressful situations. So for women, the opportunity to make new friends is far easier.

Men are in a different situation altogether. Being alone is never any fun, but men have rarely had to cope with it.

Their wives made the social arrangements. Consequently they don't know what to do and many times isolate themselves.

A role model for men is Meyer, one hundred and one. He lives in his own home by himself, makes some of his meals, and after his wife's death kept finding new things to keep busy like playing cards at a senior center, going to garage sales, and he recently went to a grandchild's wedding in New York accompanied by a young friend.

Males need companionship too. Some options are finding a poker or bridge group. Sporting events are basically a guy thing. So a guy can call up someone he knows and tell him he has an extra ticket for a baseball, or football game. There are men's organizations that help, like lunch and learn sessions and Romeo groups (Retired Old Men's Eating Organization) They meet once a week and have speakers on different topics. Guys do have friends too—but not as many as women. So, if you are a guy, you too, can network. It beats being lonely.

"Only I can change my life.
No one can do it for me"

— Carol Burnett

BORED?

Of course you are bored if you live in the north or midwest like I do, with snow and subfreezing temperatures, slick roads and heavy clouds. It's tough to get out and about. At times I too feel housebound with cabin fever.

But that's not what I'm talking about. Spring comes with lovely flowers and mild temperatures and you're still bored, with time on your hands, and nothing to do with it. You are finally retired, with a number of years left to fill. What are you going to do with them? Aging is inevitable, but you will never feel happy if you don't look at the future with enthusiasm. How long has it been since you tried something new?

So fill those hours. Get out of the house and find people to talk to with different opinions from yours who can give you new perspectives and different views to stimulate your mind. You can do it. If others can you can too.

Start each day by looking for new things to learn and try.

One of the easiest ways to lessen boredom is for seniors to find ways to volunteer and make the lives of other people better. Call a neighbor who has been ill or an old friend and make both of your days. You will be surprised how fast the day will go and there will be no time for boredom.

Here are some suggestions to try:

* Rent or download a movie and invite some people over
* Invite a new acquaintance to attend a musical program
* Attend programs at your local library
* Join a singing group
* Learn a new hobby
* Take a bus trip to a local gallery or historic site
* Go frequently to the closest Senior Center

Is there is something you hadn't gotten to do in decades? Be bold. Try something new, you will never be bored.

"You are never too old to set another goal or dream a new dream"

— C.S. Lewis

FABULOUS CENTENARIANS USE CHUTZPAH

How you age is not dependent on your genes, according to the World Health Organization. That's good to know. Only 25% of your longevity depends on your genetics, while the other 75% is dependent on external and environmental factors. Few of us live in harsh conditions that would affect our longevity. For us, to a large extent it is our own lifestyle that ultimately will impact the length of our years.

There are over 77,000 centenarians in the USA. The number is growing. Did they all live to be one hundred solely because of good genetics? No. Virtually none of them had long-lived parents. Something else was at work. Is long life a good thing? It depends on your health, and what you do with those years.

If you retire at age sixty-five what are you going to do with the rest of your life? One of my friends I met in the retirement community where I live is my role model. She is everyone's role model. She was born in Russia when Nicholas II was czar. You would never guess her age was one hundred-four by looking at her. She will never let you see her unless she is fashionably and fastidiously dressed, with her makeup applied just so. Her memory is incredible—she remembers everything and everyone. She is a superb pianist and skillfully plays for any organization that asks her—by ear! She practices two hours every day. She still plays at weddings and programs.

Regina started a career as a social case worker for Jackson County welfare. For many years she was a volunteer and was President of several organizations. She spends her days helping others by sending cards, making jokes and visiting friends. She knows what is happening in politics and sports and will give you her opinion authoritatively on almost anything newsworthy. She gives friends and staff their marching orders. That's chutzpa and enjoying life. She is amazing.

Time-wise, Gertrude, is up on Regina. She is one hundred and seven, and still lives in her home. She stopped driving when she was one hundred and two. Yes, she passed her test at 100 year old and renewed her drivers license. She proudly framed it on her wall. Until last year at age one hundred and six, she was still in a cardio exercise class twice a week, lifting small weights. She still enjoys volunteering and being around people. She credits her longevity to keeping busy. Now that's quite a role model for you!

Ida Keeling was the first woman to complete the 100-yard dash at age one hundred. At age one hundred three she broke records and received the ESPY certificate of excellence in Sports Performance. How did she celebrate? With push-ups!

In 2019 a record 13,000+ athletes from nearly every state in America traveled to Albuquerque N.M. to participate in National Senior games. One of the most inspiring moments came when one hundred and three year-old Julia "Hurricane" Hawkins set another incredible record for the 50-meter dash, smashing the record for women in 100-104 in the process. What an inspiration for her determination and passion for life!

Judge Robert Sweet, was a revered federal judge in Manhattan, New York. In his seventies he embarked on a very interesting hobby, ice skating that helped him relieve the tensions in his career.. At age 92 he was still doing his amazing figure skating with never a bone-breaking fall.

Seniors in their nineties are still teaching classes, running corporations, dancing and writing books. Take Adele Choquet, who at ninety six is teaching yoga classes. Mathilda Klein at ninety four is dancing up a storm. You can see her on Youtube.

So what's the point of all this? The point is that more and more people are living one hundred years and beyond. You may have a lot more years ahead than you might think. These centenarians can do it. So can you.

"When grandparents enter the door, discipline flies out the window."

— Ogden Nash, poet

THE PLUSES OF BEING A GRANDPARENT

Despite all the trials of seniorhood, one of the blessings is being a grandparent, or even a great-grandparent, and grand-aunts and-uncles. The little kids are wonderful. Of course they grow up to be people and that's another story.

Family life isn't what it used to be. Divorce, interfaith marriage, and separation by distance all put on stresses. Remarriage often creates blended families, and that can be tricky. Rivalry among children of two families may be open or lurking below the surface. Some keep score and feel they are losing.

With a blended family there can easily be four sets of grandparents instead of the normal two. So if this is your situation, in order to enjoy your grandkids as fully as possible, here are some thoughts.

It takes time for the new blended family to adjust. A grandparent needs to be sensitive to the process. When you are a long distance grandparent you may want to help with various problems as they arise—provided, of course, that your help has been invited. Luckily, Skype or Face-Time can let you deal with situations face-to-face. And of course, if, hopefully, there is no problem to discuss, you can actually see and visit with your grandkids—almost, but not quite as good as being there. When you are using the computer, make it a point to ask lots of questions—it shows the grandkids that you really care about them. And listen to them—really listen—without criticism. Some love to hear geezer stories, which they absolutely find impossible to conceive, such as living in a world without computers or television.

A grandparent's words of love can make a child feel like the most important one who ever lived. When grandchildren live in town you are so lucky. Even if you're one thousand miles apart, there are other ways to keep in touch besides electronics.

Kids adore getting mail addressed to them personally. In addition to holiday and birthday cards, long-distance grandparents can send photos of themselves and video tapes of bedtime stories.

When you don't have grandchildren of you own or they live far away there is a way to become a surrogate grandparent that will benefit you and the children and the family that you adopt."Surrogate Grandparents USA" on

Facebook has more than 2.500 members, thus enabling grandparents and grandchildren to connect. Aunts and uncles might look for surrogate grandchildren. So can divorced people, and singles that have never had children, or other family members who live a long distance from their children.

Joyce from Olathe Kansas told me that she contacted her church for a family that lived close by her home. She said, "I missed going to the kids' schools and seeing their concerts, going to the library with them, having my grandkids come for dinner, so I signed up as a surrogate grandparent. The mom I ended up connecting with had lost the grandparents who raised her, and her husband had lost his parents, too."

Esther from Kansas City says, "They're not our grandkids. And we don't take the place of their grandparents. But we share a very special bond that only these two generations can really understand. It allows us to pour out some grandparenting love and savvy on adorable kids who really appreciate it."

"Happiness is that state of consciousness which proceeds from the achievement of one's values."

—Ayn Rand

ETHICAL WILL

Every life has meaning. Everyone has life experiences that should be memorialized. Every life is a history lesson. Leaving money and property to your family is great. But those aren't the only assets you can give them. An asset of enormous value is an ethical will—a written document of your life, your values, your belief system, your life lessons, your hopes for their future. You don't have to be a gifted author. Anyone can do it. All it requires is honesty.

Along with explaining your values, the journal of your life experiences will astonish them. There is so much about you they don't know. The world is changing so rapidly that now they will find it almost impossible to believe what things used to be like. You did not grow up in just a world without computers. It was a world without air conditioning, without dishwashers or washing machines. It was a world without so many wonderful things they now take for granted.

Your life story may fascinate them. They will find it astonishing that there once was a world in which women never swore. And men never swore in the presence of women, where marvelous movies had neither obscenities nor nudity nor bathroom scenes. A world where a handshake was more binding than any contract a lawyer could draw up.

Share with your family what was important in your life and how you hope that their lives will reflect kindness, love and family.

Only by writing your life story can your family begin to have a real understanding of where you came from and what life has taught you.

Spend time talking to individual grandkids with your hopes for their futures. Putting your values on paper, who you are and how you lived your life gives your family the knowledge of how you want to be remembered. My own mother made a recording of her background and what was important to her in life. She was ahead of her time.

Your world was totally different from their's. Perhaps they will view you with more respect—perhaps gain insights that will prove valuable to their own lives.

"The best thing about growing older is that it takes such a long time."

— Bob Hope, comedian

YOU'RE NEVER TOO OLD TO WRITE A BOOK

You're never too old to write a book. My husband, who is ninety, just had two new historical novels published. They're well reviewed, too.

These days, everybody writes books. There are about a million new titles published every year. With print on demand and publishing via internet, just about anyone can get a book out there. Because of that, don't expect to get rich by publishing. But that's not the point.

So what is the point? Everyone has a story to tell. You have a story. So tell it. What if you're not a very good writer? There are companies out there that can help you. In fact, you can write your book and never actually publish it. You've got the time. Your autobiography will be interesting to your family, if nobody else. I've already discussed an ethical will, but this is something more than that. Imagine if you had a manuscript written by your great-grandfather, telling all about his life and a world long since vanished?

Some people are better writers than they know. Age doesn't matter. Superb works have been produced by authors whose brain cells one would think atrophied long ago.

Examples? Read "The Invisible Wall" by Harry Bernstein, published by Ballantine books. Harry was ninety-six when the book came out. Ninety six? Unbelievable! Not only did Ballantine publish it, but the reviews were fantastically favorable. Nobody could believe a near-centenarian could write so superbly. "Where have you been all these years?" everybody asked.

So why encourage seniors to write? Because despite the massive influx of writers and manuscripts, there is always room for new, great, insightful writing. Writing has no age limit. And we all have our own unique stories to tell.

PART II

DEALING WITH COMMON PROBLEMS

SENIOR MOMENTS

Oops! Where did I Leave it? I lost my car keys. I've searched everywhere. You know what? It doesn't matter. I won't need them until I find my car!

My husband laughed until he choked when I told him I was writing about memory. I manage to lose something every day. Where did I leave it? The doctor's office? The restaurant? The beauty shop? He patiently assures me they're right here, at home, and he's always right. I'm eighty eight years old. My ninety year old husband has to supply the missing words. "Where did I put the purple stuff?" He replies, "You mean the grape juice? It's on the counter, right there."

Memory. It bothers all of us "of a certain age." When we remember to think about it. When I saw my internist recently for a checkup, I shared my concern about my daily "oops" and said fearfully, "Do you think it's Alzheimers?" He said, not the least worried, "You managed to get here on the date and time of your appointment, didn't you? You didn't get lost on the way, did you? And you are still writing articles and books. Why don't you write how you compensate for the natural memory loss you are experiencing?"

Our memory does worry us. Since I'm thinking about it, and before I forget, here are some tricks I've found extremely useful for solving the 'I've lost it!' syndrome. You don't need to learn mnemonic devices.

Find a basket for everything you routinely use—your eyeglasses, house and car keys, cell phone, pill box etc. Keep it in the exact same place. Once you're firmly in the habit of going to that exact spot, you'll always find everything there. Hey, I trained my schnauzer. I can certainly train myself.

Lost your car in the parking lot? Not any more. Just look back twice when you park it, picking up a landmark so you'll remember what row it's in. Alternately, use digital recorder, or take a picture with your cell phone or text a message to yourself. Use either one to remind yourself about anything you're afraid you might forget.

Was something on the tip of the tongue that you can't recall? Like the purple stuff? Try reciting the alphabet and when you get to the letter the missing word starts with, chances are it will pop into mind.

Put something down and can't find it five minutes later? Could you have thrown it in the trash? It happens. Pay attention! Concentrate! Visualize in your mind a detailed picture. Say it out loud. "I put my file with medical bills on the bedroom dresser." How hard is that? Focusing is the key. Worse case, if you've been absent-minded, retrace everywhere you've been. You'll find it.

Remembering names? Hopeless, probably. The real problem isn't memory, it's indifference. My husband has never been able to remember names. Never. But even at his age, if a good-looking woman is introduced to him, somehow he remembers her name. Funny how that works.

When you meet someone new, try starting a brief conversation. "Nice to meet you, Alice." Where is your hometown, Alice?" "How long have you been here, Alice?" The system works. Sometimes. As a fallback, exchange calling cards, or write down the person's name as quickly as you can, jotting down as many details as possible. Her name, of course. How many kids and grandkids? Everything you can pick up about them. If you don't write it down, it vanishes in a nanosecond after you stop visiting with them. Carry the notebook with you. When you meet again, she'll be astonished and flattered at everything you remember, particularly since she has already forgotten everything about you.

Did I do it? Did I turn off the oven? Did I lock the door to the house? Did I put the garage door down? When you leave the house, just say out loud two or three times, "I'm turning off the oven. Check. "I've taken my pills." Check.

"I shut the garage door." Check.

All of us seniors joke about our loss of short term memory, but of course it's no joke at all. The solution for most things is to write everything down. So there you have it. It's not rocket science. It's mostly common sense, really. The trick is just to do it.

"If you ask what is the single most important key to longevity, I would say it is avoiding worry, stress and tension. And if you didn't ask me I'd still say it."

— **George Burns, comedian**

STRESS, SCHMESS

Stress and anxiety run high in our lives. As we age, it seems more difficult to cope. Family and longtime friends die. Physical symptoms generate mental and emotional fears.

Janet, a counselor, describes some of the ways people deal with their problems. There is "the Ostrich," who puts her head in the sand and by ignoring the problem thinks it will go away. She hopes by acting helpless, someone else will solve her problem for her. She does not learn to face reality or responsibility and develop her own abilities.

Then there is "the Blamer." Every thing is somebody's else's fault. This doesn't go very far in actually solving the problem. Moreover she never sees her own behavior as possibly being part of her problem. And the stress and anxiety don't go away.

And "the Complainer," is the worst of them all. I've talked about this type in different contexts. Bottom line, nobody likes a complainer. And kvetching or complaining solves nothing. The trouble doesn't go away.

You'll notice a pattern. The Ostrich, the Blamer, and the Complainer are all passive. Janet suggests an active approach. Ask your primary doctor for a referral to whomever he thinks would be best qualified to help you.

The most important questions you must ask are to yourself. "Is this really my problem? "Do I have control?" If the answer is "NO" then let it go. Think philosophically, "What Is, Is." Let it go. You cannot solve every problem.

Here are a few of Janet's suggestions that may be useful in dealing with stress and anxiety:

* Take deep breaths when you feel anxiety coming on.
* Get enough sleep
* Keep a diary of feelings that trigger your stress
* Talk to a friend who is a good listener
* Take a walk outside, exercise at a gym or get a trainer
* Listen to music
* Have a massage
* Prayer to a higher being may be helpful

* Read a good book

* Watch a funny movie

* Take advantage of relaxation and meditation tapes you can download

If Janet's self-help suggestion don't work then seek a professional psychologist, psychiatrist or counselor. If money or lack of insurance is a problem, try the nearest Mental Health Center.

"Gratitude is the healthiest of all human emotions. The more you express gratitude for what you have, the more likely you will have even more to express gratitude for."

— Zig Ziglar

POSITIVE THINKING WITH A JOURNAL

A gratitude journal! What is it all about? It is a diary to focus your attention on the positive things in your life. Studies suggest that people who are habitually grateful are happier and more optimistic. Consequently, one very useful device is using a journal to "count your blessings."

I was talking to Marian the other day. She has kept a journal for over five years. She informs me that writing in her journal three times a week has had a significant impact on her happiness.

Amazing! She offers some of her tips free of charge! She suggests one of the keys is to be as specific as possible about a particular person or thing for which you are grateful. Record those events that are unexpected. Write in your journal the date and at least one to three sentences about something you are thankful for that day.

As you write, try to see good things as "gifts." Try to relish those gifts you've received. Don't simply take them for granted. Commit yourself to a regular time and do it at least three times a week. Reading the previous entry the first thing every day helps to have "an attitude of gratitude." It is also helpful to finish each day thinking about the things you are grateful for. Say them out loud. By transferring our emotions to paper, rather than bottling them up inside, we can actually "see" our feelings. We can step back—and become a witness to those feelings—rather than reacting to them. Perhaps chart a new course whenever necessary. A journal is frequently a best friend because it allows you the opportunity to be open about your life.

Research shows that being grateful changes the brain in the direction of calmness and wellbeing. So turn your attention to the good things in life. In noticing happy things we can build a way to counterbalance what's painful. Give it a try.

"The best way to find yourself is to lose yourself in the service of others"

— Mahatma Gandhi

WIN BY VOLUNTEERING

I know. I know. Volunteering is supposed to be altruistic. It's not supposed to be about what you get out of it. It's supposed to be about what you give. But what in the world is wrong with a win-win situation?

So you're bored. I get that. Time on your hands. Hundreds of T.V. channels available at your fingertips and nothing on the TV worth watching. You have books, but your eyes are tired after about a half-hour of reading.

But you can volunteer. It sounds easy. But for some, it isn't. Not that they don't want to be useful, but they are reticent. For those—and you may be one of them—it can take a great effort to go out to do something that will help others. But once you've started, you probably won't quit. The golden glow that comes from volunteering is certainly rewarding.

Let me introduce you to Sandi. She has been volunteering for more than fifty years. Winning many awards over those years, and she more than earned every single one of them. When asked why she has done it, she says "the only answers I can give is that volunteering is a matter of conscience—a way to express appreciation for life and humanity, which has nothing to do with religious practice or educational goals. It makes your life all about people. The reason to volunteer is to participate in how to make life better."

Sandi spends much of her day at a retirement care facility, helping residents stay open to trying new things. The essence of her work, she says, is helping residents live to the fullest of their abilities and interests, making it not feel like a nursing home, or a place where old people go to die, but a living community. Volunteering actually energizes her, she says, and seeing smiles on the faces of the residents is like sunshine.

Sandi isn't unique. Carol has been doing mentoring through her friendship with a number of young people. She finds by sharing her skills and caring she can provide guidelines for helping them mature. Thankfully, the world is filled with Sandi and Carol. Join the crowd!

Volunteering is good for your mind and body, providing benefits for both mental and physical health. It helps counteract stress, anxiety and anger. It is said that volunteering is even better for you than exercising.

I hope that is true as I don't enjoy exercising. As a bonus, getting out of the house and doing something helpful puts you in an environment where you will meet new people and, with luck, make new friends.

"We must find time to stop to thank the people who make a difference in our lives"

— John F. Kennedy

MENTORING: HELP A CHILD SUCCEED

Carol, who I just mentioned told me that you can help shape a child's future for the better by empowering them to achieve. The best part is, it's actually a lot of fun and one of the most rewarding volunteer jobs you could possibly imagine. YouthFriends is a national program of volunteers for caring adult role models from the community who volunteer with young people in schools, grades K-12. The goal is to help students achieve success, both academically and socially. What could be more rewarding than that?

Carol was a mentor for 4th and 5th graders. The goal was to get to know the child and become their adult friend and to help the child deal with whatever issues were causing the child to be unhappy or difficult to deal with in the classroom. Teachers arc the ones who recommended the children to be part of this program. In some cases, the relationship lasted just for one year. In other cases, the mentor and child continued for several years.

Her favorite experience was with a fourth grader named Anoop. At their first meeting, he told Carol that everyone, including the teacher said he was "annoying." Truth is, he was! He said he tried to get attention, but was very unpopular with the kids. Academically, he was not progressing much. Throughout the year their relationship grew. At the end of the year he drew a map with "Ups and Downs." The map ended on a high experience and when he was asked what it stood for, he happily said that he finally had a best friend. It wasn't a child in his class, but it was Carol! Their friendship continued for four years through middle school. He was capable of many things including piano recitals where he excelled and joining a chess club at school. His attitude was no longer of a loser.

Carol's experience gave her enormous pleasure. You too, can be a part of the rewarding life as a mentor, if you give it a try it's a win-win experience.

"There is nothing in the world so irresistibly contagious as laughter and good humor."

— **Charles Dickens**

LAUGHTER —IT HELPS, AND ITS FREE

Free is a good price. You've always heard that laughter is the best medicine, but don't throw away your pills yet. Still whatever can be done to improve your health without a prescription can't be bad. When you laugh, you are helping your immune system and blood pressure. It helps your mood. It alleviates stress, depression, anxiety while bolstering self esteem. So keep cheerful friends close. Grouches and kvetches pull you down. Laugh together.

My friend Maurine is an expert regarding a phenomenon I'd never heard before—Laughter clubs that use Laughter Yoga. That's right, Laughter Yoga.

She explained that Laughter Yoga is a new twist on an ancient practice which combines unconditional laughter—without relying on jokes or comedy, by using yoga breathing. It is a group activity involving maintaining eye contact with others and promoting childlike playfulness. In most cases, this leads to real and contagious laughter. Does this sound strange? Science has proved that the body cannot differentiate between your simulated laughter and real laughter. Laughter Yoga commences with breathing exercises, and because of group dynamics progresses until laughter flows like a valve turned to the 'on' position. It triggers the release of endorphins, prompting overall relaxation and increasing blood flow. It's effect can last for days. The technique allows seniors to achieve hearty laughter without cognitive thought. Different, but true.

In the mid 1990s, Dr. Madan Kataria developed Laughter Yoga based on the concept that voluntary laughter could provide the same benefits as externally produced laughter. Laughter Yoga has spread worldwide, sparking the creation of Laughter Yoga Clubs where people gather and practice. You do not have to master any of the traditional yoga postures. There are over eight thousand clubs in sixty-six countries. Sebastian Gentry, CEO of the American School of Laughter puts it in the context of laughter wellness. Many senior centers offer classes. So check it out.

"Loneliness is my least favorite thing about life. The thing that I'm most worried about is just being alone without anybody to care for or someone who will care for me."

— Anne Hathaway

EATING WITHOUT A COMPANION

Dr. Roni Beshears, a nutritionist, says that one of the the biggest challenges for seniors is lack of companionship at meal time. Dining alone magnifies loneliness and in turn can suppress appetite and lead to poor eating habits.

She emphasizes that with a good mindset and healthy attitude eating alone does not have to be a lonely experience. She suggests that instead of dining alone "why not start a supper club." Obviously eating out every night is out of the question. But how about once a week, either rotating homes or going out to a restaurant? Or how about inviting a neighbor to eat with you? It can be potluck, or you can pick up something at your local supermarket deli. Few people turn down an invitation to dinner.

If your local senior center has food service—usually lunch—go there. Almost certainly at least a few will be dining alone, so ask them if they would like company.

Many seniors feel the way you do. Give it a try. If you are lucky, you might find a congenial friend. During the course of the year, your church or synagogue has events where meals are served. Normally seating is open, so pick a spot and you will find new people.

These suggestions work, but that still leaves times when you find yourself eating alone, and you probably don't eat with good nutritional habits. Whole books are written on proper food and diets. If you can't cook for yourself sign up for Meals on Wheels and have meals delivered. Apply for SNAP (Supplemental Nutrition Assistance) federal food benefits if income eligible.

Dr Beshears suggests that you create an environment that makes mealtime pleasurable. How? Play some music. In other words enjoy your own company.

"My eyesight is not nearly as good. My hearing is probably going away. My memory is slipping too. But I'm still around."

— John Wooden

PHYSICAL CHANGES

VISION

Macular degeneration and dry eyes may interfere with reading. In order to have enlarged print, Large Print books are often available at the library. When my eyes get tired and dry I enjoy listening to auditory books on my computer or

You can apply to the Library of Congress for talking books. The program for an audio reader is free to those who have limited sight. There are several text-to- speech programs that scan material and reads it aloud for you. One program is the Pearl Reading Camera that brings blind and low vision people portable access to printed material. The folding camera connects to your computer and can snap a picture of your reading material and begins reading it aloud instantly.

HEARING

If your hearing is limited, the government can provide you with CaptionCall telephone service. It looks like a small T.V. so that you see the message that the person is saying on the display. Call 1-877-557-2227. There's no charges for Caption Call. On your own T.V. you can have closed caption for movies or programs so that you can read the words and not miss out. Ask a friend to turn it on for you.

"The woods are lovely, dark and deep. But I have promises to keep, and miles to go before I sleep."

— Robert Frost

SLEEP

Older adults who don't sleep well are more likely to suffer from depression, attention and memory problems, excessive daytime sleepiness and more nighttime falls.

Many studies suggest adequate exercise and meditation during the day may help you sleep at night. Playing soft music may help you too. Relaxation exercises can be purchased on C.D's and some are available for free on the computer. Reading a book helps make you feel relaxed, as does calming music, or keeping a journal to record worries before you retire. Take a warm shower and a massage from a partner. On your to-do list, check off tasks completed plus goals for tomorrow, then let them go out of your mind.

Cognitive-behavioral therapy (CBT)is a form of psychotherapy that addresses the behavior before bedtime as well as changing the ways of thinking that keep you from falling asleep. It also focuses on improving relaxation skills and changing lifestyle habits that impact sleeping patterns. Sleep disorders can trigger emotional health problems such as anxiety, stress, and depression. Cognitive therapy is an effective way of treating the underlying problem rather than just the symptoms. In fact Harvard Medical School studies found CBT was more effective at treating insomnia than prescription medications and has no side effects.

"If we could give every individual the right amount of exercise, not too little or too much, we would have found the safest way to health."

— **Hippocrates**

EXERCISE: A MENTAL SUPERPOWER TO AVOID FALLS

Stop! Don't turn the page. I know what you are thinking. You're thinking "ugh" at the very mention of exercise. You're a senior and never exercised that much when you were younger. So why am I pestering you now? Because after speaking to a number of physical therapists I became convinced exercise is essential for seniors of all ages. According to them, exercise can mean the difference between remaining independent or requiring assistance of others for even the most routine activities of daily living. Stretching can improve your flexibility and moving freely will make it easier to tie your shoes. One additional important benefit to exercise is that it helps perk up your mood and reduces depression.

Classes such as Chair Yoga, Tai Chi and Water Aerobics are designed to maintain muscle strength, joint flexibility, endurance and balance. According to the National

Institute on Aging, with exercise you will stay healthier longer. You may prevent a number of diseases like diabetes, and delay osteoporosis. It can reduce pain associated with arthritis.

Although some people may have limited mobility, it is important that they continue to maximize what they can do. Most exercise can be adapted and benefited from, if done either while seated or even supine in bed.

One of the most serious problems for seniors is a fall causing a broken hip or pelvis. Often the fall will result in need for a wheelchair or scooter for the remainder of your life. Dizzy spells result in bad falls. Balance and strengthening is available at many senior and rehabilitation centers. Take advantage of it!

Many falls occur in your home where you trip over your own feet or a rug on the floor. Having the right shoes can often avoid a fall. One place we don't think about is a fall out of bed that can cripple you. This needn't happen. Have bed rails or body pillows on each side of the frame to help prevent rolling over the edge during the night. One simple trick to prevent a person falling out of bed is to use a simple water noodle placed under the inside of the mattress pad and sheet. Use it for a reminder you are close to the edge. No need to fill it with water!

There is an important social aspect to attending a group exercise class as well. By exercising it provides the opportunity to meet new people who are working toward similar fitness goals. It can provide the motivation that one needs to exercise consistently and incorporate exercise into the daily routine. So start today, with all the benefits, what do you have to lose?

"The moment you start asking questions, you become public enemy number one."

— Richard Ojeda

FIRE YOUR DOCTOR IF YOU AREN'T HAPPY

That's right. Fire your doctor, if he or she deserves it, that is. When your internist tells you if you have more than one question you must make another appointment, it's time to leave. It happened to me. I don't go to him anymore.

Yes, Medicare makes it very difficult for doctors—it keeps lowering reimbursements, and it saddles them with mountains of paperwork. I get that. They feel they need to give you less time and to work more quickly. But, I don't have to like it. I have found that, as a general rule, it's best to find doctors at major medical centers where the physicians are working on a salary basis. They are more likely to be willing to spend the time with you that you deserve.

So use chutzpah. If necessary fire your doctor. Some doctors that you've used for decades are nearing retirement and are burned out. I don't blame them. Spending a lifetime listening to everyone's trouble would burn me out too.

If you can afford the cost you may want to consider a concierge doctor. Yes, you have to pay an annual fee for the concierge doctor. The doctor commits to being available anytime you call. Only you can know whether the doctor is worth the extra expense.

When you have a potentially serious diagnosis or the need of surgery, it is important to get a second opinion. That should be a given, but it's surprising how many don't question the findings. But doctors are not always infallible. Quite often there can be more to your problem than the first doctor you see suspects.

PART III

GETTING YOUR ACT TOGETHER

In order to carry a positive action we must develop here a positive vision.

— Dalai Lama

GETTING YOUR ACT TOGETHER

What? You haven't drawn up your will yet? Or you haven't taken a look at it for, say twenty years or so? Obviously, now is the time to get your affairs in order. First and most important, make sure someone in your family, or your lawyer, has an up-to-date list of where they can find all the needed documents—-will, insurance, assets, tax returns, real estate, automobile ownership, documents, location of safe-deposit box, trust, durable power of attorney for health care, and financial advance directive—in short, everything that may be needed in case you are no longer able to handle your own affairs, or inevitably are no longer here.

I strongly urge you to consult with an Elder Lawyer to go over everything. Quite frequently decisions you have made—or have deferred making—can have unintended legal consequences. In addition, make sure your wishes are known to your family. If you have promised certain children or grandchildren certain assets after you are gone, put it in writing to avoid arguments among your heirs.

You need a living will for your future health needs. Do your homework about advanced care planning. There are state agencies that can help you.

You may need an advocate to check on you and if necessary, speak on your behalf. This may involve a binding agreement to bequeath assets in exchange for providing oversight.

These are among the things an Elder Lawyer will do for you:

* Estate planning, including review and update of your will and trusts
* Transfer assets to avoid impoverishment if spouse enters a nursing home.
* Process Medicare and SocialAssist in securing survivor benefits
* Make sure you receive the proper benefits of health law and insurance

"My biggest hobby is hanging out with my family and kids."

— Joel Osteen

RETIREMENT WITH A NEW HOBBY

Wow! Do I have an idea for you! It's an old one and nearly forgotten. But if you are a senior orphan and if you're housebound, this could keep you busy and energized without having to leave your home.

Ham radio. Really? Yes! The American Relay League. wireless proclaims Amateur Radio (ham radio)as a popular hobby and service that brings people together. People use ham radio to talk across town, around the world and even into space, all without cell phones. It's fun, social, educational and can be a lifeline during times of need. Sounds like a relic from the 30's. It definitely isn't.

Larry S, at eighty eight, has been in ham radio since 1960 when he became licensed. For the past twenty years he has managed an informational email service for his fellow hams, with approximately 2100 subscribers to WOAIB in the Kansas City area. Visit him at LarryListinfo and you'll get all the information you need, including how to obtain a license.

Larry told me, "I started at the age of twenty-nine. There are no age barriers. We just licensed a young lady of ten. One of the great benefits to seniors is the easy mixing of all ages. This definitely has kept me young." There are many ham ladies. To learn how to get started and what equipment you will need, go to www.kchamlink.org/home/first-steps. It isn't all that expensive.

Ham radio is a wonderful way for people to make new friends. It is a special hobby to introduce to grandchildren or to any other important children in your life. They will be fascinated to be able to connect with you and share interesting thing that are going on in both of your lives. There are 695,000 ham radio licenses in the United States. A great hobby in retirement can be a functional emergency option. What a rewarding way to spend your time!

"Animals are such agreeable friends - they ask no questions; they pass no criticisms."

— George Eliot

EVERYONE CAN USE A PET

There are many benefits of pet ownership for seniors according to my neighbor psychologist Dr. Ed, who has a dog called Pippa. Everyone needs a pet like Pippa. Dr. Ed, says Pippa never criticizes him, is always friendly and doesn't use your credit card. Pets help reduce stress and can comfort us even more than our friends and spouses. Pets give us their unconditional love. They don't judge us. We are never alone when our pet is with us. Of course if we have a dog, we need to walk him, but walking is exercise and it gets us out of the house. It is great fun when we meet up with another dog lover and our pets interact on the ends of a leash.

Pets can have a positive effect on depression and loneliness. Petting your cat or dog feels good for both of you. If you can't have a pet where you live try one of the new robotic pets. Technology is wonderful! You can now buy a wonderful little dog or cat that is absolutely lifelike. A special little companion, responding to sound and touch. One dog I found from Ageless Innovation Joy could be a great little companion. He responds to sound motion and touch. Nuzzle his face and he turns towards you. His barks, pants, and yawns are so realistic its hard to realize he isn't really a dog. He even has an on, off, and mute switch so he can be silenced if you choose. It's the next best thing to a live animal without the responsibility of taking him outside for a walk on bitter winter days, and no vet bill!

A well trained dog that you have bonded with can save your life. There are many stories of dogs that have alerted people when their owner is ill or having problem. One such story is

Terry McGlade, a U.S. Marine, suffers from PTSD and seizures after being wounded by an IED in Afghanistan. When he had a seizure, Major, a trained rescue dog, knew exactly what to do: He called for help. Not by whining or barking, but by pawing at McGlade's iPhone.

Major called 911 by repeatedly stepping on the phone's screen for several seconds, alerting concerned dispatchers who eventually heard McGlade having a seizure in the background. In an interview with Fox & Friends, McGlade says the dog called 911 a total of ten times.

Dr Ed suggests if you are considering adding a dog to your family, it's best to check with a veterinarian before doing so. Even if you had a dog like a Jack Russell, previously, if you have a sedentary lifestyle now, it may not be wise to invite a really energetic dog into your life. There are a number of breeds, including, of course, some rescue dogs, that can co-exist with you just fine. Best to ask your vet first before adopting.

Having a dog is a responsibility but needn't be taxing. The routine of caring for a pet can give structure and purpose to daily life. Maybe you don't always want to get out of bed, but your pet wants you to, and isn't that a good thing? Sure, you need your pet. But your pet needs you, too. It is very satisfying to take care of another living thing.

"Music gives a soul to the universe, wings to the mind, flight to the imagination and life to everything."

— Plato

MUSIC IS GOOD FOR THE BRAIN

If you want to keep your brain engaged throughout the aging process, listening to or playing music is a must. It provides a total brain workout. There is a national music program for retired seniors called New Horizon International Music Association. Check it out.

The idea is for adult beginners, and some that played in school, to have an entry point to be comfortable playing or learning a new instrument. Active participation in music fills important needs. To challenge intellectual activity, the need to be a contributing member of a group, and the need to have exciting events in the future.

A woman, retired and widowed, joined the band to have something to do. Now she doesn't know what she would do without it. This comes at a time in life when you have the time to devote to it. When you join the band, you stick with it. According to her, not many people drop out. It's something that holds you. Of course one of the big pluses is that it gives you an opportunity to meet new people.

How about the Barbershop Harmony Society? Barbershop singing has been around forever. Larry P. lives in my retirement village. A widower, he finds that his VLQ (Very Large Quartet)helps him ward off loneliness. Currently, his group Homeward Bound has eight men with two singing each of the four parts at the same time. Thus if they have a gig if one is unable to perform there is a backup. He is now eighty-eight, the youngest in the group. He is known as "the kid" The oldest is ninety six years old.

In addition to his singing in his group Larry took up playing the trombone at age seventy-three. This helped expand his cognitive skills, learning a completely new instrument. He plays it well, too.

If you don't fancy getting that involved, listening to music, singing, playing an instrument can reduce anxiety, lower blood pressure and sometimes even reduce pain as well as improve sleep quality, mood, mental alertness and memory. Not bad for something we enjoy anyway. How often can something we like be good for us?

"Grow old along with me! The best is yet to be,
The last of life, for which the first was made
Our times are in His hand Who saith "A whole
I planned, Youth shows but half; trust
God: see all, nor be afraid!"

— **Robert Browning**

RELIGION IS IMPORTANT TO SENIORS

In the United States, religious congregations have been graying for decades, and young adults are now much less religious than their elders. Recent surveys found that younger adults are far less likely than older generations to identify with a religion, believe in God or engage in a variety of religious practices.

But this is not solely an American phenomenon: lower religious observance among younger adults is common around the world, according to a new analysis by Pew Research Center surveys conducted in more than 100 countries and territories over the last decade.

Several Mayo Clinic studies report religious people literally live longer. This has been corroborated by eighteen studies. Less cardiovascular disease, hypertension and lower blood pressure are found among the religious.

Many older people report that religion is the most important factor enabling them to cope with physical health problems and life stresses (e.g. declining financial resources, loss of a spouse or partner). A hopeful, positive attitude about the future helps one remain motivated to appreciate their life.

Religion may provide us the means to cherish the blessings of age and realize the gift of years and to live these years well. A positive and hopeful attitude about life and illness, predicts improved health outcomes and lower mortality rates.

A sense of meaning and purpose in life, which affects health behaviors and social and family relationships can become more meaningful through faith.

PART IV

"Computers, and software yet to be developed, will revolutionize the way we learn"

— Steve Jobs

GRANDMA'S A TECHIE

That's right. I'm a techie. Well, almost. A lot closer to being a techie than most eighty-eight year olds. You can become computer savvy at any age. If I, with five great grandkids, can, there's no reason you can't do it, too.

My friend, Irene, an expert in teaching the use of the computer, tells seniors that the internet is a huge library that's always open. The computer opens up a whole world, right at your fingertips.

An internet connection, she says, is an amazing tool. You need not understand how the computer works, and it is almost impossible to damage, unless you spill a beverage on it or drop it. You can wander around websites, which is called "browsing" or use a "search engine" to look for specific topics. Even if you don't have your own computer, free usage is available at many libraries and community centers. Some people are intimidated by the computer. Don't be. It won't bite. But it can open up a whole new world to you.

I became a beginner at age eighty five. I learned to use a "smart" cell phone. My granddaughter Amanda put me on Facebook and is telling all her friends "Grandma is a techie, she writes me text messages and tweets."

Well, truth of the matter is that perhaps I'm not really a techie, but I'm farther along than I'd ever dreamed--so far along that people actually call me for help. Between you and me, most of the time I can't help them, but amazingly enough sometimes I can.

Of course what I could do at that point was pretty basic stuff. These computers are miracle machines, and can do thousands of times more than we usually ask. Websites can be your newspaper, weather reporter, dictionary or encyclopedia. You can find music and radio stations, language lessons, recipes, the text of a song or the value of your vintage objects. You can email, make online bill payment, buy plane tickets, do a variety of puzzles, the uses are endless.

I got hooked on social networking and set myself set up on Facebook. I discovered social networking isn't just for teenagers. Over twenty-seven million people fifty-five and over use social networking. You can, too. If you're a housebound seniors it's particularly wonderful; it lets you maintain contact with old friends and create new ones. It's a magic carpet for finding old school chums you never thought you'd hear from again.

One of the great uses of computers is Skype. It is a camera built into the computers that enables you to see and talk to friends and family, for free. I can see our twin great grandkids, who, by the way, are the cutest you'll ever see. Skype helps them remember us between visits. One of my friends in Kansas City watched a wedding of her grandson in New York via Skype because she had just come home from the hospital and couldn't travel. If you don't use it you don't know what you are missing!

Irene cautions, use common sense when you're on the computer. Hackers are out there and no one is immune. There are scams sent to consumers. You should rarely respond to personal information requests on the computer. Never give usernames or passwords to anyone. Don't click on links written in an email if you don't know the sender. Nothing in this world is ever perfect.

COMPUTER MAGIC

Irene had a few more suggestions for how to use your computer:

* Communicate via Facebook, Skype or FaceTime
* Find new cyber friends
* Manage your finances
* Download movies
* Listen to music
* Share photo albums
* Shop online
* Work on puzzles
* Read book and movie reviews

CYBER FRIENDS

I met Dorothy seven years ago, on line. She got my attention with her email, dorothy@itsnevertoolate.com She is an amazing women. For more than three decades she has been a spokesperson for people enjoying their second fifty years. An army wife, Dorothy raised six children when she was widowed suddenly at the age of forty-eight. She reinvented herself and is a broadcaster, newspaper columnist, author, who keeps audiences laughing. We have become real pen pals—or computer pals might be more accurate. You will enjoy her. Dorothy has chutzpah. Check out her web site.

BLOGGING

As long as we're talking about computers, let's talk about blogging. I'm sure you've heard the term, but might not know what it is. A blog is a discussion topic that you post on your website, communicating what you are thinking or what you think might be of interest. It's incredible how much blogging goes on now.

It's never too late to blog. Ruth Hamilton died two months before her one hundred and tenth birthday. She had been blogging until the very end. She had been married to a major league baseball player, was the first woman to host a radio show, and had been elected to the New Hampshire legislature. A remarkable woman, eager to embrace anything new.

I scoured the web for best blogs for seniors. You will find them in the appendix. They give the latest breakthroughs in health care, traveling, fashion or just having a great laugh.

For seniors who are housebound and cannot easily use the computer because of arthritis, low vision or other difficulties, there are devices such as talking software and speech recognition software that permit you to communicate. If you say you are bored or have time on your hands now that you are retired, it's your own fault. Buy yourself a computer, learn to use it. Take classes at the local community centers and libraries. What better use do you have for your time?

MORE ABOUT TECHNOLOGY AND AGING

Technology is changing our lives. Many advances are already in place. Even with physical limitations there are alternate ways of coping. With smart home technology you can go hands free with a voice assistant from Amazon echo or Google home. A speaker lets you play music by voice commands, dims your lights, turns up the temperature on your thermostat, automates a fan or controls a coffee maker, all without lifting a finger.

Be sure to acquire a device to wear around your neck or wrist notifying an alarm company in an emergency—usually a slip and fall. There are a number of companies that you can choose from.

We will soon live surrounded by high tech sensors, voice assistants and automated pill dispensers. There's a "companion" robot to ward off loneliness called 'Lovot' that rolls around looking for hugs. Who needs people anymore?

Apple watches can monitor blood pressure and heart rate for your doctor. It also provides a fall alert and SOS signal. The Dexcom G6 watch can check your glucose level at a glance. You can avoid pricking your finger, plus it is covered by some insurance plans.

Ring video doorbell ring.com or nest.com lets you see, hear and talk to someone at the door whether you are home or away. Truly helpful to my neighbor Judy, who has a walker.

Worried about memory problems? IGuardFire.com will turn off electric and gas stoves at preset times. Most ovens have timers, but this works for stovetops.

Hopefully, all these intelligent machines will remember we're still the boss.

Of course none of these are free. The price ranges from a few dollars to several hundreds, but if you feel any might be worthwhile for you, you can look them up on line or check them out at home improvement stores.

"Once you stop learning, you start dying"

— Albert Einstein

LEARN SOMETHING NEW- IT'S NEVER TOO LATE

Albert Einstein was right. By now you've noticed a recurring theme in this book. The theme is time. By and large seniors have a full day that needs to be filled. This book is about ways to use your time. It's easy to do, but it does take effort. It also requires breaking old habits of thinking, which can be tough.

There's no reason not to make an effort to learn things. There are college level classes for free with no tests or grades at many junior colleges and senior centers. Free lectures and community events abound at libraries. Why not attend? Check newspaper listing and neighborhood bulletin boards for schedules.

Join a book club or discussion group. Don't hesitate to ask your local library or bookstore for help in finding a group. Many senior centers have book clubs. Another good way to meet new people.

A trusty computer can open doors to learning with the mere click of a couple of keys. Great courses are provided by National Geographic. Each course is taught by an award winning scholar, who shows up on your computer. Many courses are available at $35 per course. Just dial 1-800-832-2412 for a catalog. People can learn a language on line, or view tutorials to learn to play instruments.

Brains, like muscles, atrophy with disuse. You can create neural pathways until you die. At the very least you can challenge your brain with mind games and puzzles.

YOU THINK YOU'RE ALONE, BUT YOU'RE NOT

Just because you live alone doesn't mean that you are alone. If you already have friends you can call on, that's great. But if not, nothing is going to drop into your lap without a little effort on your part. You need to actively create a network—it needn't be large—of people you can call on for help, if needed.

If you are unable to drive, become familiar with local transportation. Check out local agencies and learn how to contact Uber or Lyft. It's really easy. With a cell phone you just put in their number. Check them out now. Some day you might need one on very short notice, and rather than being under the gun to make a last-second choice, know well in advance which one would best serve your needs, and how to contact them.

Be sure you have designated someone who will make medical decisions for you should you suddenly become incapable of making your own choices. This should be done through a health care proxy durable power of attorney, which will also permit your financial affairs to be taken care of. Make sure a family member knows where the document is.

Check out caregiver resources in your community again to the time when they become needed. Friends may have suggestions, or check Senior Agencies Bluebook in your area.

When there are family problems that cannot be resolved it is important to call in professionals. If the problems cannot be resolved, it's time to accept things that you cannot change.

Using chutzpah means not hesitating to ask for help when you need it. There are many sources in your community that can provide what you may need. Check the appendix for suggestions.

"The greatest challenge to any thinker is stating the problem in a way that will allow a solution."

— Bertrand Russell

ONE LAST THOUGHT

When life challenges us with body and mind changes, we have a choice. We can feel sorry for ourselves and kvetch, "Why is this happening to me?" The far better option is to ask "what can I do to help myself?" The answer is that you must take control of your life. Isolation makes you miserable. There's plenty to keep you active all day, but you're the only person that can do it. Be bold, stop being afraid to try something new. Focus on what you can do and not what you have lost.

Loneliness is a state of mind. It is a challenge to make new friends as you grow older. Women and men with close friends and strong social support tend to sleep better, heal faster, experience less depression, and stave off cognitive decline as they age. And these are the facts.

Life is going to give you all types of challenges the longer you live. You need to have a plan and adapt to the changes. Make the most of the gift of years. Never give up. You are still here, while so many people you've known are not.

One thing is certain. Your family will be enormously thankful that you're self-reliant. You will be a role model for them when they become seniors. Best of luck for making the most of your time for all the days to come.

ACKNOWLEDGEMENTS

I thank my husband of sixty seven years, who has been there for me with all our reinventions in life. You have always been supportive and looked at the positive side. Our three daughters and grandchildren gave me insight into how the younger generations views aging. Thank you to my forever old friends who were ready to be there when I needed them. You became part of my family.

I appreciate the help from friends and professionals whose work are cited in this book. Their own life experience has given significant direction of the content. Because of their help this manuscript has grown from sharing their life with me.

Those include Dr Roni Roth Beshears, Dr.Ed Christopherson, Cheryl Choikhit, Sandra Ettlinger, Marian Kaplan, Sandi Lerner, Dena Moss, Maurine Pachter, Regina Pachter, Larry Poisner, Janet Price, Judy Revare, Dr. Blanche Sosland, Larry Staples, Irene Starr, Gertrude Stern, Dr. Wally Weber, Dorothy Wilheim, and Carol Yarmo.

I am most grateful for the Centenarians in my retirement home, who are role models for living life to the fullest.

APPENDIX

COMPUTER WEB SITES

National

agenet.net

ncoa national council on aging

pioneer network.net

gu.org generations united

SOCIAL NETWORKS

facebook.com

genkvetch.com

growingbolder.com

itsnevertoolate.com

third age.com

timegoesby.net

theroamingboomers.com

RELIABLE HEALTH INFORMATION

AARP

Alzheimers Association

diabetes.org

medlineplus.gov National Library of Medicine

ahrg.gov Agency for Health care research

hopkinsmedicine.org

mayoclinic.org

ON LINE MAGAZINES

American Senior magazine.com

Elderhostel International

EldersAction Network

Grandparenting.org

Longevity.com

Next avenue.com

Seniornet.com

Senior Times.com

PODCASTS (AUDIO RECORDINGS)

agingintoradio

growingbolder.com

it'snevertoolate.com

SOB Spunky Old Broad

BOOKS FOR SENIORS

The Gift of Years, Joan Chittister

Everything I've Learned About Change, Lesley Garner

Project Renewment: First Model For Career Women, Helen Dennis, Bernice Bratten

Grow Your Best Life: It's An Inside Job, Jenifer Johnson

Banishing Bullying Behavior: A Call to Action, Blanche Sosland, Ph.D.

SUPPORT GROUPS

eldersaction.net

Connect2Affect.org

SeniorCorps.org

seniorplanet.org

FOR HOUSEBOUND SENIORS

Those who have difficulty getting around or handling routine tasks can benefit from the following devices: Voice-enabled assistant: Popular products like the Amazon Echo or Google Assistant will let you operate compatible smart home products with voice commands.

These devices can also play music, read audiobooks, make calls, set timers and alarms, provide reminders for medications and appointments, check traffic and weather, answer questions and more — all by voice commands.

Medication management: Seniors on a complex medication schedule can benefit from a smart medication tracking system like the PillDrill to remind you when pills are due. Abbot Freestyle glucose monitor alerts you about your glucose without pricking your finger. Apple watch series four can check heart electrical impulses and has added fall detection.

FOOD DELIVERY SERVICES

These services will bring the food and goodies to your house. Some charge a minimum of $35. Others are free, you simply give a tip to the person who brings it to your door. Here are several national services:

Instacart instacart.com/grocery-delivery

Doordash

Amazon Prime Membership

Grub Hub

Costco Grocery Service

Uber Eats

Made in the USA
Columbia, SC
04 May 2022